The Best Things About 'Layer Cakes':
Non-Fattening • Sugar Free • No C

Friends & Flowers
pages 4 - 5

Portugal
pages 6 - 7

Peace on Earth
page 8

Cranberry Wishes
page 9

Posh
page 10

Hemming House
page 43

11 Beautiful Quilts from 10" x 10" Squares

Smores Snowmen
page 44

Fresh Squeezed
page 45

Natural Garden
pages 46 - 47

Birchwood Lane
pages 48 - 49

Wee Play Rainbow
pages 50 - 51

Friends & Flowers

pieced by Donna Perrotta
quilted by Julie Lawson

Basic shapes and bold primary colors make this a perfect quilt for a nursery, playroom or child's bedroom. Simple piecing provides an excellent start for beginners and makes this quilt a choice candidate for the many community service projects which endeavor to supply quilts for hospitals and homeless shelters.

instructions on pages 12 - 15

Friends & Flowers
'Layer Cake'

Portugal

pieced by Donna Arends Hansen
quilted by Julie Lawson

Adventure awaits around every corner of your holiday in Portugal. It's sure to be sunny, breezy and warm wherever you make this pretty quilt featuring the curving stems of stylized roses.

instructions on pages 35 - 38

Portugal
'Layer Cake'

Peace on Earth

pieced by Betty Nowlin
quilted by Julie Lawson

Carefully planned color placement allows the play of light and dark to emerge when you stand back from this intriguing quilt, reminding us that it's the contrast of differences that creates harmony and peace.

instructions on pages 23 - 24

Peace on Earth
'Layer Cake'

Cranberry Wishes

pieced by Lanelle Herron
quilted by Sue Needle

When the seasons turn to sumptuous hues, the wild geese begin their annual migration. Find them here preparing to take flight amidst 9-patch blocks. This graphic quilt is a celebration of the delightful ways to combine traditional blocks.

instructions on pages 41 - 42

Cranberry Wishes
'Layer Cake'

Posh
Fast and Easy BIG Blocks Quilt

pieced by Donna Perrotta
quilted by Julie Lawson

Totally retro! This posh design is as simple as it gets. This quilt gets its 'oomph' from the sensational swirls in the fabric while the thin strips between the rows corral the movement and give the eye a place to rest.

instructions on page 11

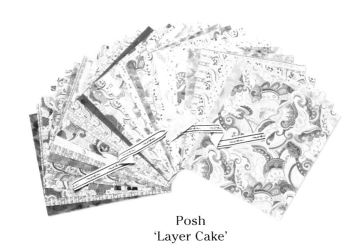

Posh
'Layer Cake'

Posh
Fast and Easy BIG Blocks Quilt

PHOTO ON PAGE 10

SIZE: 59½" x 65½"

YARDAGE:
We used a *Moda* "Posh" by Chez Moi
- we purchased 1 Layer Cake
(You'll need a total of 31 squares 10" x 10")

1 Red solid	OR	⅓ yard
5 Pink prints	OR	⅝ yard
1 Pink solid	OR	⅓ yard
5 Yellow prints	OR	⅝ yard
1 Yellow solid	OR	⅓ yard
5 Green prints	OR	⅝ yard
1 Green solid	OR	⅓ yard
5 Aqua prints	OR	⅝ yard
1 Aqua solid	OR	⅓ yard
5 Brown prints	OR	⅝ yard
1 Brown solid	OR	⅓ yard

Border #1	Purchase ¼ yard Brown
Border #2 & Binding	Purchase 1¾ yards Pink print
Backing	Purchase 3½ yards
Batting	Purchase 68" x 74"

Sewing machine, needle, thread

SORTING:
Set aside the following 10" squares for the blocks:
- 5 Pink prints
- 5 Yellow prints
- 5 Green prints
- 5 Aqua prints
- 5 Brown prints

Set aside the following 10" squares for sashings:
- 1 Red solid
- 1 Pink solid
- 1 Yellow solid
- 1 Green solid
- 1 Aqua solid
- 1 Brown solid

PREPARATION FOR BLOCKS:
Sashings:
Cut 5 Sashing strips 1½" x 10" from each of solid colors:
Red, Pink, Yellow, Green, Aqua, Brown.

Blocks:
Sew a solid sashing strip to the bottom of each print block, matching colors. Press.
For Pink blocks only, also sew a Red sashing strip to the top of each block. Press.

ASSEMBLY:
Arrange all Blocks on a work surface or table.
Refer to diagram for block placement and color.
Sew the pieces for each row together. Press.
Sew the rows together. Press.

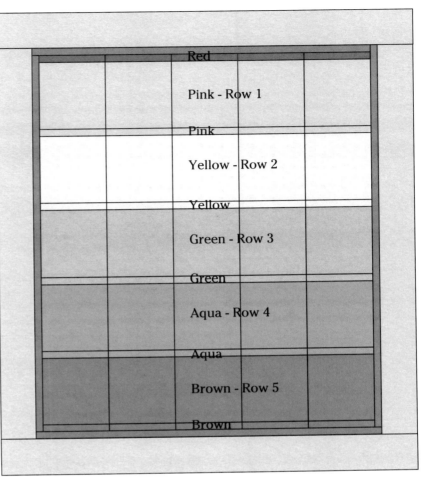

Posh
Quilt Assembly

BORDERS:
Border #1:
Cut 5 strips 1½" x 42" on the crosswise grain.
Sew strips together end to end.
Cut 2 strips 1½" x 54" for sides.
Cut 2 strips 1½" x 50" for top and bottom.
Sew side borders to the quilt. Press.
Sew top and bottom borders to the quilt. Press.

Border #2:
TIP: Cut the strips parallel to the selvage to eliminate piecing on the long borders.
Cut 2 strips 5½" x 56" for sides.
Cut 2 strips 5½" x 60" for top and bottom.
Sew side borders to the quilt. Press.
Sew top and bottom borders to the quilt. Press.

FINISHING:
Quilting:
See Basic Instructions on pages 32 - 33.
Binding:
Cut strips 2½" wide.
Sew together end to end to equal 260".
See Binding Instructions on page 34.

Friends & Flowers

PHOTO ON PAGES 4 - 5

SIZE: 49½" x 61¾"

YARDAGE:

We used a *Moda* "Friends & Flowers" by Mary Englebreit
- we purchased 1 Layer Cake
(You'll need a total of 32 squares 10" x 10")

4 Red	OR	⅓ yard
4 Blue	OR	⅓ yard
4 Green	OR	⅓ yard
3 Yellow	OR	⅓ yard
3 Stripe	OR	⅓ yard
8 White	OR	⅝ yard
2 Black	OR	⅓ yard
4 Plaid	OR	⅓ yard

Border #1   Purchase ¼ yard Black with dots
Border #2 & Binding   Purchase 1¾ yards Red print
Backing   Purchase 2⅞ yards
Batting   Purchase 58" x 70"
Sewing machine, needle, thread
8 Yellow 1" buttons (not for children)
DMC Green pearl cotton or 6-ply floss
#22 chenille needle

SORTING:

Cut and set aside the following deepest colors for sashing strips:
    2 Red
    3 Blue
    3 Green
    3 Yellow
Cut and set aside the lightest colors to make block centers:
    8 White
    4 Plaid
Cut and set aside these colors for appliques:
    1 Green
    2 Red
    2 Black
    1 Blue
Set aside 3 Stripes for Corner Squares.

PREPARATION FOR BLOCKS

Block Centers:
    Cut 8 White and 4 Plaid squares 10" x 10".

Corner Squares:
    Cut 20 Striped squares 3¼" x 3¼".

Sashings:
    Cut the following strips 3¼" x 10":
    6 Red, 9 Blue, 8 Green, 8 Yellow.

Row 1
Row 2
Row 3
Row 4
Row 5
Row 6
Row 7
Row 8
Row 9

ASSEMBLY:
    Arrange all Blocks, Corner Squares and Sashing strips
       on a work surface or table.
    Position the Corner Squares so the stripes are horizontal.
    Refer to diagram for block placement and color.
    Sew the pieces for each row together. Press.
    Sew rows together. Press.

BORDERS

Border #1:
Cut 5 strips 1½" x 42" on the crosswise grain.
Sew strips together end to end.
    Cut 2 strips 1½" x 52¼" for sides.
    Cut 2 strips 1½" x 42" for top and bottom.
    Sew side borders to the quilt. Press.
    Sew top and bottom borders to the quilt. Press.

Border #2:
Cut strips parallel to the selvage to eliminate piecing.
    Cut 2 strips 4½" x 54¼" for sides.
    Cut 2 strips 4½" x 50" for top and bottom.
    Sew side borders to the quilt. Press.
    Sew top and bottom borders to the quilt. Press.

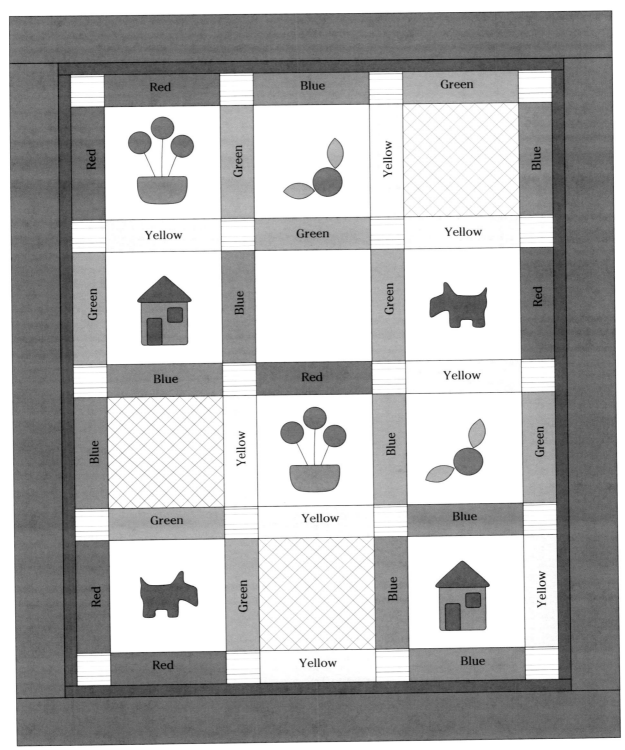

Friends and Flowers - Quilt Assembly

APPLIQUES:
Use the desired method of applique.
Trace patterns onto a template.
For Direct Applique: Fuse fabrics to Steam-a-Seam 2, then cut out fabric.
For Turned Edge Applique: Cut out fabrics leaving a scant ¼" seam allowance to turn the edges under.
Stems: Make Running Stitches with Green pearl cotton or 6-ply floss and a chenille needle.
Follow the Applique Instructions on page 33.

FINISHING:
Quilting:
See Basic Instructions on pages 32 - 33.
Binding:
Cut strips 2½" wide.
Sew together end to end to equal 243".
See Binding Instructions on page 34.
Buttons:
After quilting and binding, sew a button to each flower center.
NOTE: Do not use buttons on quilts intended for babies and young children. Embroider a center with floss.

Applique Patterns

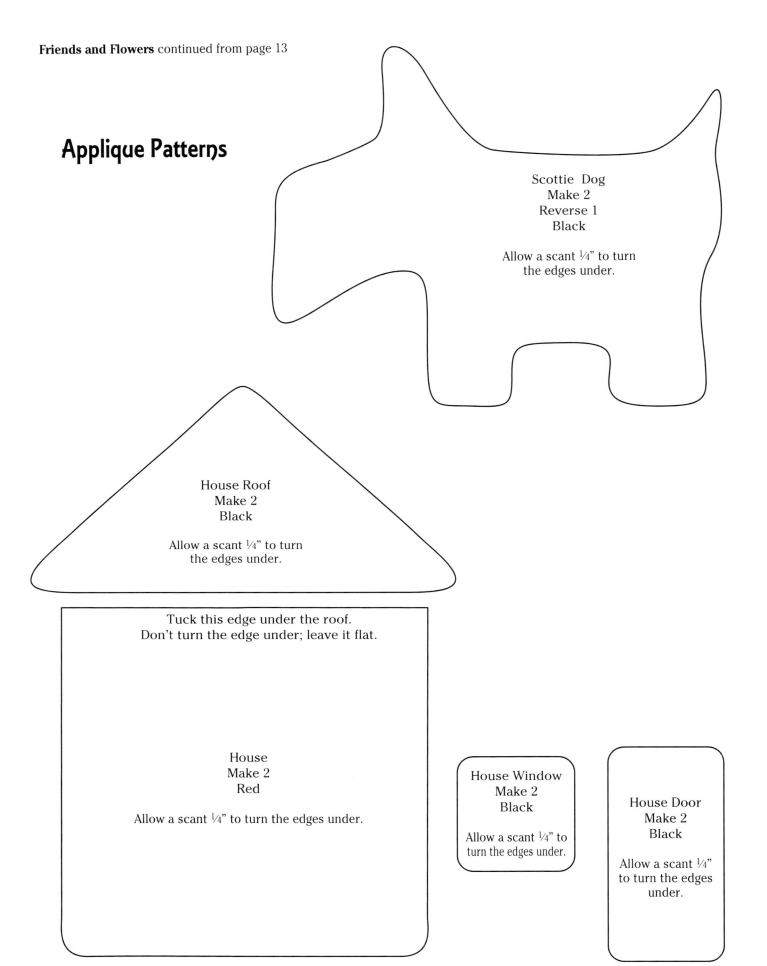

Scottie Dog
Make 2
Reverse 1
Black

Allow a scant ¼" to turn
the edges under.

House Roof
Make 2
Black

Allow a scant ¼" to turn
the edges under.

Tuck this edge under the roof.
Don't turn the edge under; leave it flat.

House
Make 2
Red

Allow a scant ¼" to turn the edges under.

House Window
Make 2
Black

Allow a scant ¼" to
turn the edges under.

House Door
Make 2
Black

Allow a scant ¼"
to turn the edges
under.

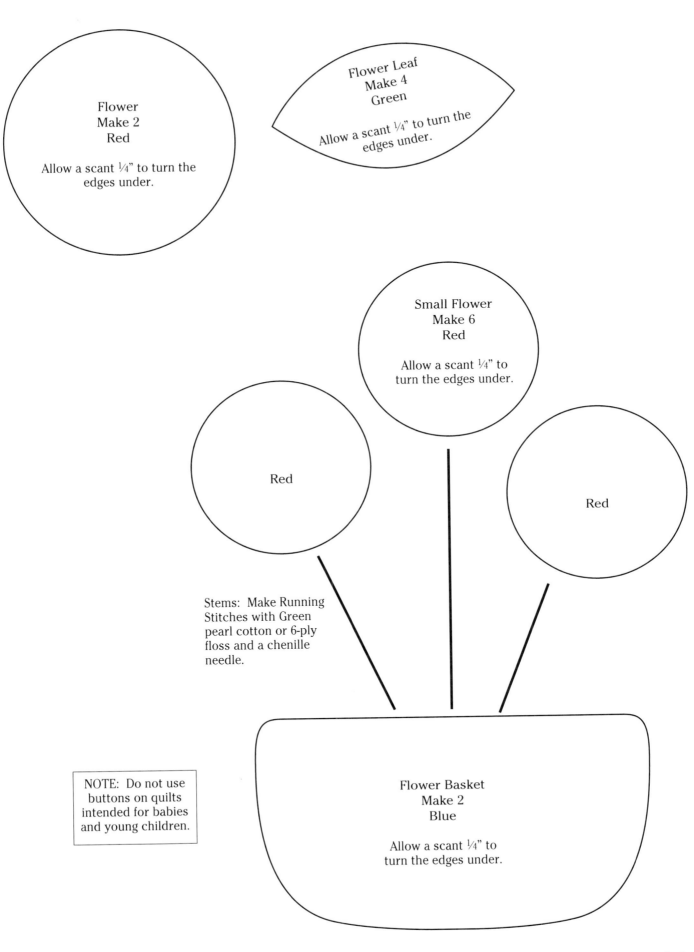

Flower
Make 2
Red

Allow a scant ¼" to turn the edges under.

Flower Leaf
Make 4
Green

Allow a scant ¼" to turn the edges under.

Small Flower
Make 6
Red

Allow a scant ¼" to turn the edges under.

Red

Red

Stems: Make Running Stitches with Green pearl cotton or 6-ply floss and a chenille needle.

NOTE: Do not use buttons on quilts intended for babies and young children.

Flower Basket
Make 2
Blue

Allow a scant ¼" to turn the edges under.

Natural Garden

PHOTO ON PAGES 46 - 47

SIZE: 46" x 54"

YARDAGE:
We used a *Moda* "Natural Garden" by Holly Taylor
  - we purchased 1 Layer Cake
  (You'll need a total of 31 squares 10" x 10")

4 Red	OR	⅓ yard
5 Tan	OR	⅝ yard
3 Dk Green	OR	⅓ yard
4 Green	OR	⅓ yard
3 Purple	OR	⅓ yard
8 White	OR	⅝ yard
4 Lavender	OR	⅓ yard

Border #2	Purchase ¼ yard Dark Green
Border #3 & Binding	Purchase 1⅓ yards Tan
Backing	Purchase 2¼ yards
Batting	Purchase 54" x 62"

Sewing machine, needle, thread

SORTING:
Cut and set aside the following 10" x 10" squares to make
    half-square triangles:
    2 Red, 3 Tan, 1 Dark Green, 2 Green, 1 Purple, 8 White
Cut each 10" square into 9 squares, 3" x 3" to make the
    following:
    16 Red, 24 Tan, 8 Dark Green, 16 Green, 8 Purple, 72 White

Each pair of squares
will <u>make 2</u>

TIP: Follow Half-Square Triangle Diagram on page 34.
HALF-SQUARE TRIANGLES:
    Pair up two 3" x 3" squares (each White with a color
        square) together.
    Draw a line from corner to corner on the diagonal.
    Sew a seam ¼" on each side of the diagonal line.
    Cut apart on the diagonal line to make 2 squares.
    Press.
    Make 144 half-square triangles.
    Center and trim each half-square triangle to 2½" x 2½".

PREPARATION FOR BLOCKS:
Cut 36 Lavender 2½" squares for the corners.
Cut the following 8½" x 8½" center squares:
    2 Red
    2 Tan
    2 Dark Green
    2 Green
    1 Purple
NOTE: Save leftover 1½" pieces to use for Top & Bottom bor-
ders.

    Refer to the Block Assembly Diagram to group the pieces
        for each block.
NOTES:
    For all blocks <u>except the center block</u>, the color of the half-
        square triangle matches the color of the center square.
    <u>The center block</u> uses a Dark Green center and Tan-White
        half-square triangles.

Each block uses 4 Lavender corner squares and 16 half-square
triangles.

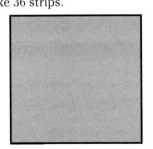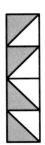

SEW BLOCKS:
    Refer to Block
Assembly diagram for placement.
    For each block, sew 4 half-square triangles (2 left and
        2 right) in a row to make a strip 2½" x 8½".
    Press.
    Make 36 strips.

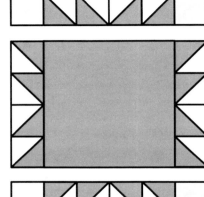

Sew a set of 4 half-square triangles to each side of the
    block center square. Press.
Each block will measure 8½" x 12½" at this point.

Block Assembly

    Sew a Lavender square to each end of the
        2 remaining sets.
    Press.
    Sew a set to the top and bottom of the block.
    Press.
    Each block will measure 12½" x 12½" at this point.

ASSEMBLY:
    Arrange all Blocks on a work surface or table.
    Refer to diagram for block placement and direction.
    Sew blocks together in 3 rows, 3 blocks per row. Press.
    Sew rows together. Press.

BORDERS:
Top and Bottom Pieced Border #1:
Cut leftover colored pieces into strips 1½" wide.
Randomly sew the strips together end to end.
    Cut 8 strips 1½" x 36½".
    Sew 4 strips together side by side to make a piece
        4½" x 36½". Press.
    Sew the piece to the top of the quilt. Press.
Repeat using the remaining 4 strips and sew the piece to the
    bottom of the quilt. Press.

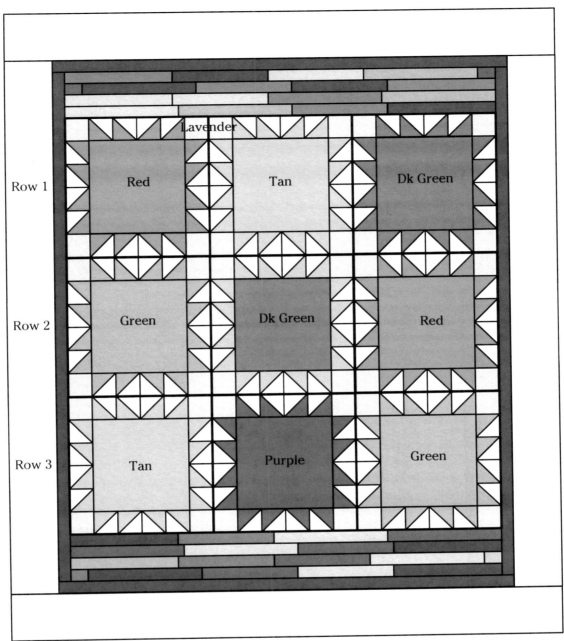

Natural Garden
Quilt Assembly

Border #2:
Cut 4 strips 1½" x 42" on the crosswise grain.
Sew strips together end to end.
    Cut 2 strips 1½" x 44½" for sides.
    Cut 2 strips 1½" x 38½" for top and bottom.
    Sew side borders to the quilt. Press.
    Sew top and bottom borders to the quilt. Press.

Border #3:
TIP: Cut the strips parallel to the selvage to eliminate piecing on the long borders.

Sew strips together end to end.
    Cut 2 strips 4½" x 46½" for sides.
    Cut 2 strips 4½" x 46½" for top and bottom.
    Sew side borders to the quilt. Press.
    Sew top and bottom borders to the quilt. Press.

FINISHING:
Quilting:
    See Basic Instructions on pages 32 - 33.
Binding:
    Cut strips 2½" wide.
    Sew together end to end to equal 210".
    See Binding Instructions on page 34.

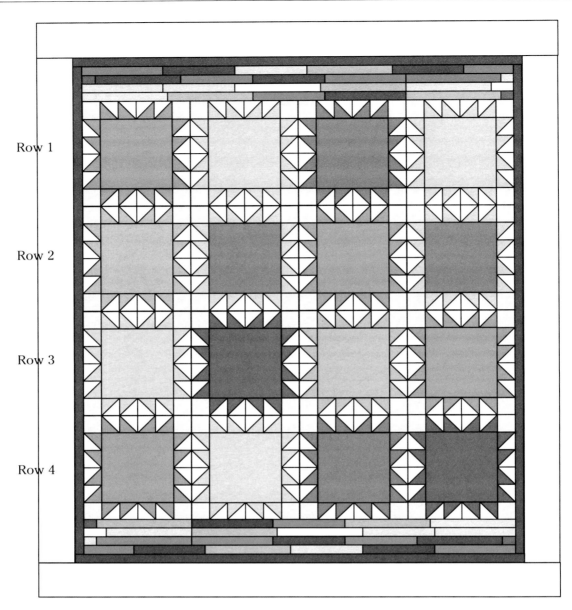

Row 1

Row 2

Row 3

Row 4

Natural Garden Variation - Big Quilt Assembly

Natural Garden

BIG Quilt Variation

REFER TO INSTRUCTIONS ON PAGES 16 - 17.

SIZE: 63" x 71"

YARDAGE:

We used 2 Layer Cake collections
    (You'll need a total of 56 squares 10" x 10")
    Increase the quantities on page 16.

Border #2   Purchase ⅜ yard Dark Green
Border #3 & Binding   Purchase 2 yards Tan
Backing   Purchase 4 yards
Batting   Purchase 71" x 79"
Sewing machine, needle, thread

MAKING BLOCKS:
Follow the basic instructions on pages 16 and 17,
increasing quantities for this large quilt.
    Make 256 half-square triangles.
    Make 64 side strips.
    Make 16 blocks.

ASSEMBLY:
    Arrange all Blocks on a work surface or table.
    Refer to diagram for block placement and direction.
    Sew blocks together in 4 rows, 4 blocks per row. Press.
    Sew rows together. Press.

Top and Bottom Pieced Border #1:
Cut 8 strips 1½" x 48½". Follow instructions on page 16.

Border #2:
Cut 2 side strips 2" x 56½"
Cut 2 top and bottom strips 2" x 51½".

Border #3:
Cut 2 side strips 6½" x 59½".
Cut 2 top and bottom strips 6½" x 63½".

Wee Play Rainbow
Fast and Easy Half-Square Triangle Blocks Quilt

PHOTO ON PAGES 50 - 51

SIZE: 57" x 66"
YARDAGE:
We used a *Moda* "Wee Play" by American Jane
  - we purchased 1 Layer Cake
  (You'll need a total of 32 squares 10" x 10")

7 Red	OR	⅝ yard
2 Lt Orange	OR	⅓ yard
2 Dk Orange	OR	⅓ yard
5 Yellow	OR	⅝ yard
6 Green	OR	⅝ yard
6 Lt Blue	OR	⅝ yard
4 Blue	OR	⅓ yard

Border #1	Purchase ¼ yard Dark Blue
Border #2 & Binding	Purchase 1¾ yards Multi stripe
Backing	Purchase 3½ yards
Batting	Purchase 65" x 74"

Sewing machine, needle, thread

SORTING:
Set aside the following 10" x 10" squares to make half-square triangles:
    4 Red
    2 Light Orange
    2 Dark Orange
    2 Yellow
    6 Green
    6 Light Blue
    4 Blue

Each pair
makes
2 squares.

 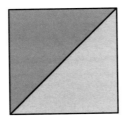

Half-Square Triangles

TIP: Follow Half-Square Triangle Diagram on page 34.
HALF-SQUARE TRIANGLE BLOCKS:
Match the following squares for the half-square triangles:
    2 pairs of Red-Red
    2 pair of Lt Orange-Dark Orange
    1 pair of Yellow-Yellow
    3 pairs of Green-Green
    2 pairs of Light Blue-Light Blue
    1 pair of Light Blue-Blue
    1 pair of Blue-Blue

  Pair up two 10" x 10" colors (refer to list above for color pairs).
  Draw a line from corner to corner on the diagonal.
  Sew a seam ¼" on each side of the diagonal line.
  Cut apart on the diagonal line to make 2 squares.
  Press.
  Center and trim all blocks to 9½" x 9½".
  Make 24 half-square triangles.

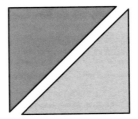 

Triangle Blocks - Cut and then Sew.

TRIANGLE BLOCKS:
Set aside the following 10" x 10" squares to make triangle blocks:
    3 Red
    3 Yellow
    1 Blue
    1 Lt Blue

  Cut each square listed above on the diagonal.
  Mix up the pieces so you get the following:
    3 Yellow-Yellow with different prints
    3 Red-Red with different prints
    1 Lt Blue-Blue
  TIP: Handle the pieces carefully to avoid stretching along
    the diagonal.
  Pair up two triangles.
  Sew a seam ¼" from the diagonal.
  Open the block and press.
  Center and trim to 9½" x 9½".

ASSEMBLY:
  Arrange all Blocks on a work surface or table.
  Refer to diagram for block placement and direction.
  Sew blocks together in 6 rows, 5 blocks per row. Press.
  Sew rows together. Press.

BORDERS:
Border #1:
Cut 5 strips 1½" x 42" on the crosswise grain.
Sew strips together end to end.
  Cut 2 strips 1½" x 54½" for sides.
  Cut 2 strips 1½" x 47½" for top and bottom.
  Sew side borders to the quilt. Press.
  Sew top and bottom borders to the quilt. Press.

Mitered Border #2:
Cut the strips parallel to the selvage to eliminate piecing on the long borders.
  Cut 2 strips 5½" x 66½" for sides.
  Cut 2 strips 5½" x 57½" for top and bottom.
Center a side border strip along each side of the quilt,
  allowing 5½" to hang off each edge for mitering.
Repeat for top and bottom border strips.
See instructions for mitered borders on page 20.

FINISHING:
Quilting:
  See Basic Instructions on pages 32 - 33.

Binding:
  Cut strips 2½" wide.
  Sew together end to end to equal 256".
  See Binding Instructions on page 34.

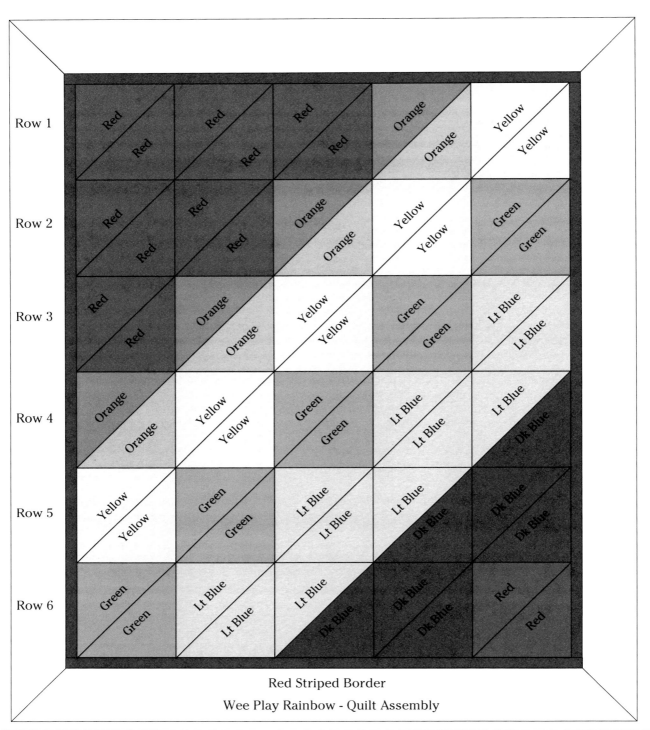

Row 1 | Row 2 | Row 3 | Row 4 | Row 5 | Row 6

Red Striped Border

Wee Play Rainbow - Quilt Assembly

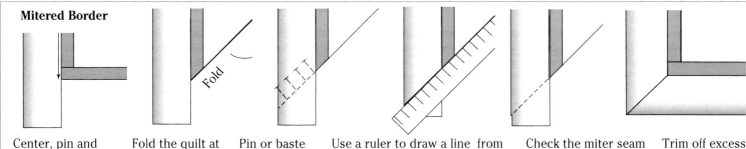

Mitered Border

Center, pin and sew borders to the sides of the quilt. Stop the seam at the corner.

Fold the quilt at a diagonal so the miter will extend from the corner outward.

Pin or baste miter seam, carefully, lining up the pattern.

Use a ruler to draw a line from the corner out to the edge of the border. Sew a seam.
TIP: I use a long stitch in case I need to rip it out and redo it.

Check the miter seam to be sure it lines up correctly and lays down flat, resew it with a normal stitch.

Trim off excess fabric underneath the corners. Repeat on all 4 corners.

Fresh Squeezed

PHOTO ON PAGE 45
SIZE: 88" x 106"
YARDAGE:
We used a *Moda* "Fresh Squeezed" by Sandy Gervais
- we purchased 2 Layer Cakes
(You'll need a total of 80 squares 10" x 10")

4 Turquoise	OR	⅓ yard
8 Dark Orange	OR	⅝ yard
12 Light Orange	OR	⅞ yard
12 Light Green	OR	⅞ yard
10 Yellow	OR	⅞ yard
20 Light	OR	1½ yard
6 Plaid	OR	⅝ yard
6 Stripe	OR	⅝ yard
2 Odd Large Stripe	OR	⅓ yard

Border #1	Purchase ⅔ yard Turquoise
Border #2 & Binding	Purchase 3 yards Dark Orange print
Backing	Purchase 5⅓ yards
Batting	Purchase 96" x 114"

Sewing machine, needle, thread

SORTING:
Set aside the following 10" x 10" squares and trim to 9½" x 9½":
  4 Stripe
  4 Plaid
  16 Light Print
Set aside the following 10" x 10" squares to make half-square triangles:
  12 Light Orange
  12 Light Green
  2 Stripe
  10 Yellow
  8 Dark Orange
  2 Plaid
  4 Light Print
  4 Turquoise
  2 Odd - Large Stripe

Each pair makes 2 squares.

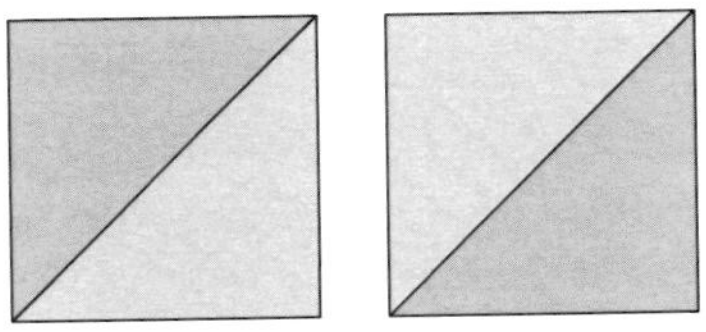

TIP: Follow Half-Square Triangle Diagram on page 34.
HALF-SQUARE TRIANGLES:
Match the following squares for the half-square triangles:
  4 pairs of Light Orange-Light Print
  8 pairs of Light Orange-Light Green
  8 pairs of Dark Orange-Yellow
  2 pairs of Stripe-Yellow
  4 pairs of Turquoise-Light Green
  2 pairs of Plaid-Odd Large Stripe

  Pair up two 10" x 10" colors (refer to list above for color pairs).
  Draw a line from corner to corner on the diagonal.
  Sew a seam ¼" on each side of the diagonal line.
  Cut apart on the diagonal line to make 2 squares.
  Press.
  Center and trim all blocks to 9½" x 9½".
  Make 56 half-square triangles.

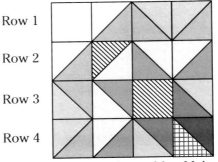

Row 1
Row 2
Row 3
Row 4

Large Block Assembly - Make 4

LARGE BLOCKS:
Refer to the Block Assembly diagram and photo for placement.
For each block, sew 16 blocks together:
  4 rows of 4 squares each.

Row 1:
Lt Print - Lt Print/Lt Orange -
Lt Orange/Green - Green/Lt Orange

Row 2:
Lt Print/Lt Orange - Stripe/Yellow -
Dk Orange/Yellow - Yellow/Dk Orange

Row 3:
Green/Lt Orange - Yellow/Dk Orange -
Diagonal Stripe - Turquoise/Green

Row 4:
Green/Lt Orange - Yellow/Dk Orange -
Green/Turquoise - Plaid/Odd

Each block will measure 36½" x 36½" at this point.
Make 4.

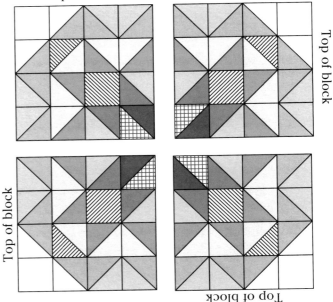

Top of block

Assemble 4 Large Blocks

ASSEMBLY:
  Arrange the 4 Large Blocks on a work surface or table.
  Refer to diagram for block placement.
  Sew blocks together in 2 rows, 2 blocks per row. Press.

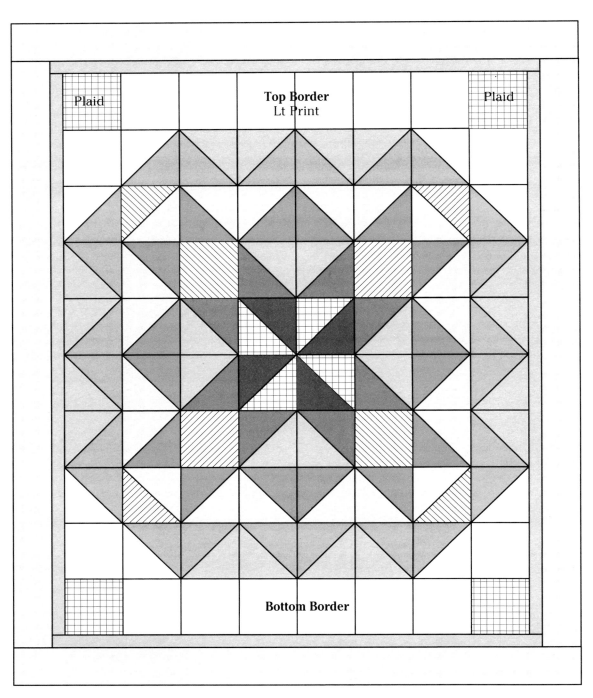

Fresh Squeezed - Quilt Assembly

BORDERS:

Top and Bottom Borders:
 Sew 1 Plaid - 6 Light Print - 1 Plaid
  to make a strip 9½" x 72½".
 Make 2.
 Sew these borders to the top and bottom.
 Press.

Border #1:
Cut 9 strips 2½" x 42" on the crosswise grain.
Sew strips together end to end.
 Cut 2 strips 2½" x 90½" for sides.
 Cut 2 strips 2½" x 76½" for top and bottom.
 Sew side borders to the quilt. Press.
 Sew top and bottom borders to the quilt. Press.

Border #2:
Cut the strips parallel to the selvage to eliminate piecing on the long border.
 Cut 2 strips 6½" x 94½" for sides.
 Cut 2 strips 6½" x 88½" for top and bottom.
 Sew side borders to the quilt. Press.
 Sew top and bottom borders to the quilt. Press.

FINISHING:
Quilting:
 See Basic Instructions on pages 32 - 33.

Binding:
 Cut strips 2½" wide.
 Sew together end to end to equal 398".
 See Binding Instructions on page 34.

Peace On Earth

PHOTO ON PAGE 8
SIZE: 88" x 106"
YARDAGE:
We used a *Moda* "Peace on Earth" by 3 Sisters
- we purchased 2 Layer Cakes
(You'll need a total of 80 squares 10" x 10")

22 Tan	OR	1⅔ yards
16 Blue Gray	OR	1⅛ yards
12 Brown	OR	⅞ yard
16 Light Green	OR	1⅛ yard
14 Red	OR	1⅛ yard

Border #1	Purchase ⅔ yard Green
Border #2 & Binding	Purchase 3 yards Tan print
Backing	Purchase 5⅓ yards
Batting	Purchase 96" x 114"

Sewing machine, needle, thread

SORTING:
Set aside the following 10" x 10" squares and trim to 9½" x 9½":
  16 Tan

Set aside the following 10" x 10" squares to make half-square triangles:
  6 Tan
  16 Blue Gray
  12 Brown
  16 Light Green
  14 Red

Each pair makes 2 squares.

TIP: Follow Half-Square Triangle Diagram on page 34.
HALF-SQUARE TRIANGLES:
Match the following squares for the half-square triangles:
    2 pairs of Tan-Blue Gray
    14 pairs of Blue Gray-Red
    12 pairs of Brown-Light Green
    4 pairs of Tan-Light Green

Pair up two 10" x 10" colors (refer to list above for color pairs).
Draw a line from corner to corner on the diagonal.
Sew a seam ¼" on each side of the diagonal line.
Cut apart on the diagonal line to make 2 squares.
Press.
Center and trim all blocks to 9½" x 9½".
Make 64 half-square triangles.

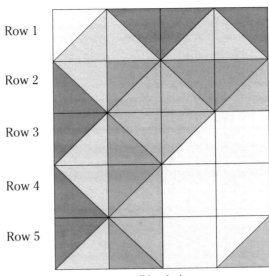

Row 1
Row 2
Row 3
Row 4
Row 5

Block A

PREPARATION FOR BLOCKS
Refer to the Block Assembly diagram for placement.
For each block, sew 5 rows of 4 squares. Press.
Block A:
Make 2
    Row 1: Tan/Blue - Blue/Red - Red/Blue - Blue/Red.
    Row 2: Red/Blue - Brown/Green - Green/Brown - Brown/Green
    Row 3: Red/Blue - Brown/Green - Green/Tan - Tan
    Row 4: Red/Blue - Brown/Green - Tan - Tan
    Row 5: Red/Blue - Brown/Green - Tan - Tan/Green
Each block will measure 36½" x 45½" at this point.

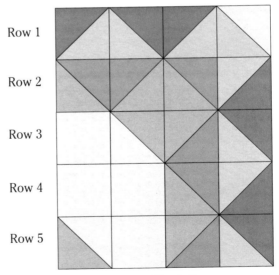

Row 1
Row 2
Row 3
Row 4
Row 5

Block B

Block B:
Make 2
    Row 1: Red/Blue - Blue/Red - Red/Blue - Blue/Tan
    Row 2: Green/Brown - Brown/Green - Green/Brown - Blue/Red
    Row 3: Tan - Tan/Green - Green/Brown - Blue/Red
    Row 4: Tan - Tan - Green/Brown - Blue/Red
    Row 5: Green/Tan - Tan - Green/Brown - Blue/Red
Each block will measure 36½" x 45½" at this point.

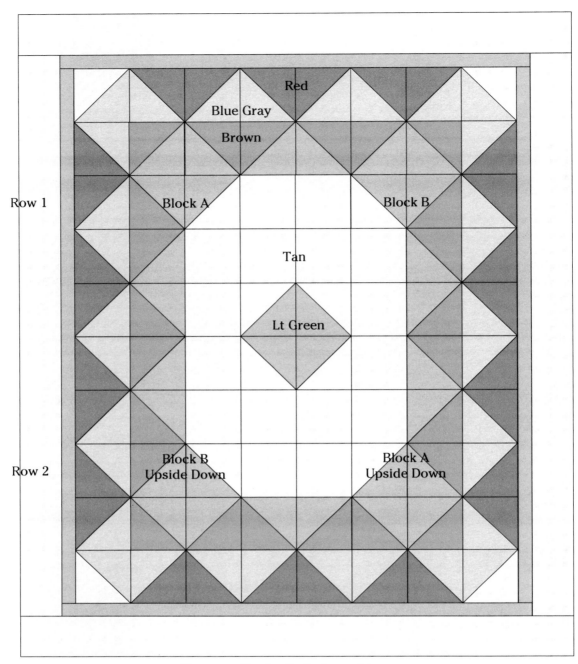

Peace on Earth - Quilt Assembly

ASSEMBLY:
Arrange all 4 Blocks on a work surface or table.
Refer to diagram for block placement and direction.
Sew blocks together in 2 rows, 2 blocks per row. Press.
Sew rows together. Press.

BORDERS:
Border #1:
Cut 8 strips 2½" x 42" on the crosswise grain.
Sew strips together end to end.
Cut 2 strips 2½" x 90½" for sides.
Cut 2 strips 2½" x 76½" for top and bottom.
Sew side borders to the quilt. Press.
Sew top and bottom borders to the quilt. Press.

Border #2:
TIP: Cut the strips parallel to the selvage to eliminate piecing on the long borders.
Cut 2 strips 6½" x 94½" for sides.
Cut 2 strips 6½" x 88½" for top and bottom.
Sew side borders to the quilt. Press.
Sew top and bottom borders to the quilt. Press.

FINISHING:
Quilting:
See Basic Instructions on pages 32 - 33.

Binding:
Cut strips 2½" wide.
Sew together end to end to equal 398".
See Binding Instructions on page 34.

Birchwood Lane

PHOTO ON PAGES 48 - 49

SIZE: 80" x 96"

YARDAGE:

We used a *Moda* "Birchwood Lane" by Holly Taylor
- we purchased 2 Layer Cakes
(You'll need a total of 80 squares 10" x 10")

4 Cream	OR	⅓ yard
8 Dark Brown	OR	⅝ yard
14 Medium Green	OR	1⅛ yards
8 Brown	OR	⅝ yard
16 Tan	OR	1⅛ yards
14 Dark Green	OR	1⅛ yards
16 Maroon	OR	1⅛ yards

Border #1	Purchase ⅝ yard Maroon
Border #2 & Binding	Purchase 3 yards Dark Brown
Backing	Purchase 6⅙ yards
Batting	Purchase 88" x 104"

Sewing machine, needle, thread

SORTING:

Set aside the following 10" x 10" squares and trim to 8½" x 8½" for top and bottom rows and Block corners:
- 10 Medium Green
- 4 Brown
- 4 Dark Brown
- 14 Dark Green

Set aside the following 10" x 10" squares for star centers:
- 4 Medium Green
- 4 Brown

Cut each 10" square into 4 squares 4½" x 4½".

Set aside the following 10" x 10" squares to make half-square triangles:
- 16 Tan
- 16 Maroon
- 4 Dark Brown
- 4 Cream

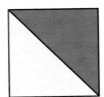

Each pair makes 2 squares.

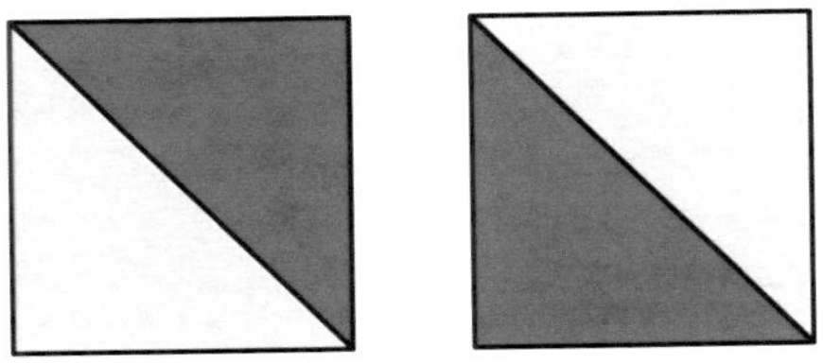

TIP: Follow Half-Square Triangle Diagram on page 34.

MAROON/TAN HALF-SQUARE TRIANGLES:
Cut each Maroon and Tan 10" square to 9" x 9".
Pair up two 9" x 9" colors (a Tan with a Maroon square).
Draw a line from corner to corner on the diagonal.
Sew a seam ¼" on each side of the diagonal line.
Cut apart on the diagonal line to make 2 squares.
Press.
Center and trim all blocks to 8½" x 8½".
Make 32 half-square triangles.

Each pair makes 2 squares.

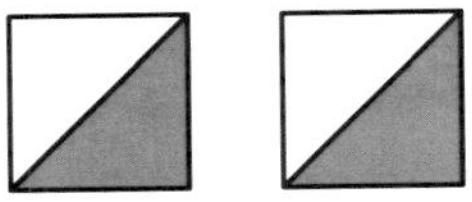

TIP: Follow Half-Square Triangle Diagram on page 34.

CREAM/DARK BROWN HALF-SQUARE TRIANGLES:
Cut all 10" Dark Brown and Cream squares into 5" x 5" squares.
Pair up two 5" x 5" colors (a Dark Brown with a Cream square).
Draw a line from corner to corner on the diagonal.
Sew a seam ¼" on each side of the diagonal line.
Cut apart on the diagonal line to make 2 squares.
Press.
Center and trim all blocks to 4½" x 4½".
Make 32 half-square triangles.

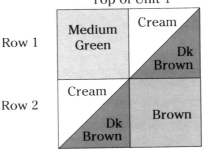

Unit 1 Diagram

PREPARATION FOR BLOCKS:

Unit 1:
Refer to the Unit 1 Diagram for color placement.
Row 1:
Sew a Medium Green 4½" square to a Cream-Dark Brown half-square triangle. Press.
Row 2:
Sew a Cream-Dark Brown half square triangle to a Brown 4½" square. Press.
Sew the rows together. Press.
Make 16 units.

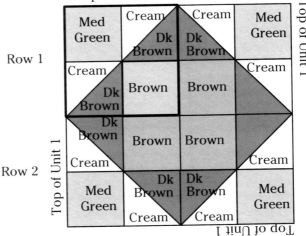

Block Center - 4 of Unit 1

Sew Block Centers:
Refer to the Block Center Diagram (rotate 4 of Unit 1).
Sew 2 rows with 2 units per row. Press.
Sew the rows together. Press.
Make 4.

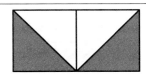

Unit 2 - Top & Bottom for Blocks A and B - Make 16

Unit 2 - For Blocks A and B:
Refer to the Block Side Diagrams for color placement.
Sew 2 Maroon/Tan half-square triangles together.
Press.
Make 16.

Unit 3 - Block Sides for A with corners:
Refer to the Block Side Diagrams for color placement.
Sew a **Dark Green** square to each end of a Unit 2.
Press.
Make 4 pieces 8½" x 32½".

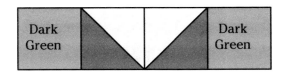

Unit 3 - Block A Sides - Make 4

Unit 4 - Block Sides for B with corners:
Refer to the Block Side Diagrams for color placement.
Sew a **Medium Green** square to one end
    and a **Dark Green** square to the other end.
Press.
Make 4 pieces 8½" x 32½".

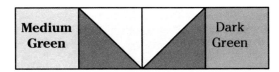

Unit 4 - Block B Sides - Make 4

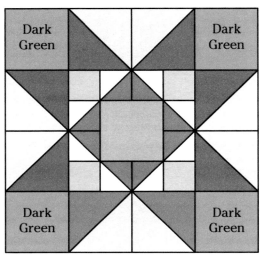

Block A - Make 2

Block B - Make 2

SEW BLOCKS:
Refer to the Quilt Assembly Diagram for color placement.
For all 4 Block A & B Centers, sew a Unit 2 to top & bottom.
Make 4. Press.

Block A:
Sew a Unit 3 to each side of the block.
Make 2. Press.
Each block will measure 32½" x 32½" at this point.

Block B:
Sew a Unit 4 to each side of the block.
Make 2. Press.

Unit 5 - Top and Bottom Rows:
Sew the following 8½" squares in a line to make a piece 8½" x 64½":
Press.

Repeat for the bottom row.
Press.

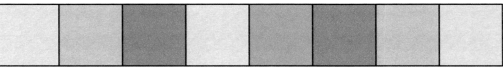

Med Green - Brown - Dark Brown - Med Green - Dark Green - Dark Brown - Brown - Med Green
Unit 5 - Top and Bottom Rows

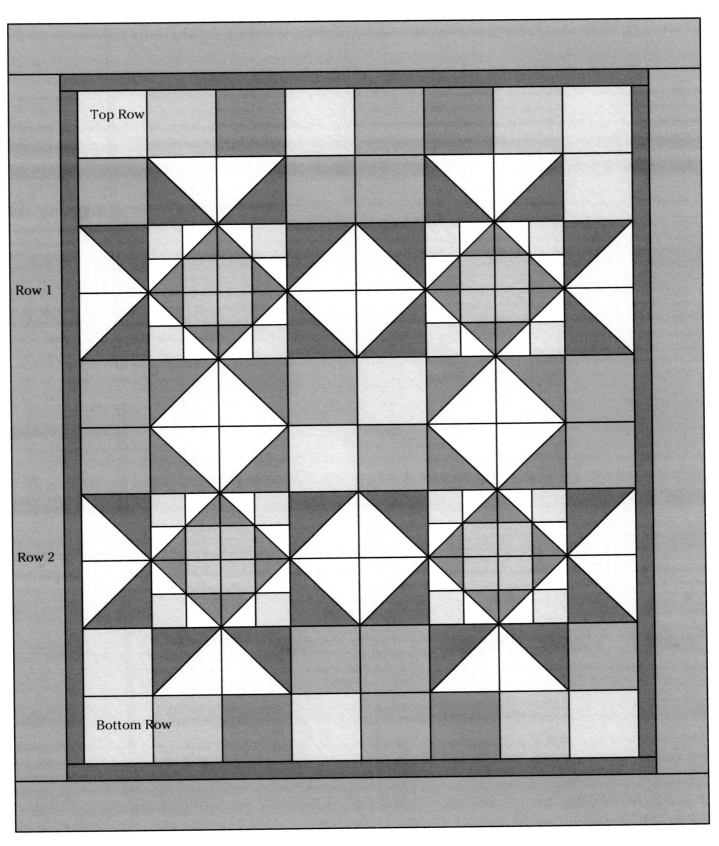

Top Row

Row 1

Row 2

Bottom Row

Birchwood Lane - 2 Layer Cakes
Quilt Assembly

Birchwood Lane - 1 Layer Cake
Quilt Assembly

Birchwood Lane
Variation

REFER TO INSTRUCTIONS ON PAGES 25 - 28.

SIZE: 49½" x 74"
We used 1 Layer Cake.
YARDAGE:

Border #1	Purchase ⅓ yard Maroon
Border #2 & Binding	Purchase 2 yards Dark Brown
Backing	Purchase 4⅝" yards
Batting	Purchase 58" x 82"

Make 2 Block A's. Sew together. Press.
Make 1 Unit 5 into a piece 8½" x 64½".
Cut into 2 strips 4¼" x 64½".
Sew to each side of quilt center.

Border #1:
Cut 2 strips 1½" x 64½" for sides.
Cut 2 strips 1½" x 42" for top and bottom.
Border #2:
Cut 2 strips 4½" x 66½" for sides.
Cut 2 strips 4½" x 50" for top and bottom.

ASSEMBLY:
Arrange all Blocks on a work surface or table.
Refer to diagram for block placement.
Sew blocks together in 2 rows, 2 blocks per row.
Press.
Sew rows together. Press.

BORDERS:
Top and Bottom Rows:
Sew a row to the top and bottom of the quilt. Press.
Border #1:
Cut 8 strips 2½" x 42" on the crosswise grain.
Sew strips together end to end.
Cut 2 strips 2½" x 80½" for sides.
Cut 2 strips 2½" x 68½" for top and bottom.
Sew side borders to the quilt. Press.
Sew top and bottom borders to the quilt. Press.

Border #2:
TIP: Cut the strips parallel to the selvage to eliminate
piecing on the long borders.
Cut 2 strips 6½" x 84½" for sides.
Cut 2 strips 6½" x 80½" for top and bottom.
Sew side borders to the quilt. Press.
Sew top and bottom borders to the quilt. Press.

FINISHING:
Quilting:
See Basic Instructions on pages 32 - 33.

Binding:
Cut strips 2½" wide.
Sew together end to end to equal 362".
See Binding Instructions on page 34.

Smores

PHOTO ON PAGE 44

SIZE: 90" x 91"

YARDAGE:

We used a *Moda* "Smores" by Me & My Sister
- we purchased 2 Layer Cakes
(You'll need a total of 75 squares 10" x 10")

12 Purple	OR	⅞ yard
12 Aqua	OR	⅞ yard
12 Pink	OR	⅞ yard
12 Green	OR	⅞ yard
3 Tan	OR	⅓ yard
24 White	OR	1⅔ yard

Border #1   Purchase ⅝ yard Purple
Border #2 & Binding   Purchase 3 yards Aqua
Backing   Purchase 6½ yards
Batting   Purchase 98" x 99"
Buttons & Beads   16 ⅞" for eyes, 24 ⅞" for shirt, 8 - 6mm x 19mm
                   Black rice beads for mouth (not for children)
Sewing machine, needle, thread

PREPARATION FOR BLOCKS:

Cut and set aside the following:
24 White print squares for the snowmen.
Tip: Plan to use the busiest and/or darkest print Whites for the body
    and the lightest Whites for the head.

BACKGROUND COLORS:
NOTE: Each snowman is surrounded by its own background color.
Cut the following:
From 8 each (Purple, Aqua, Pink and Green), cut the following:
    5" x 10" strips (16 Purple, Aqua, Pink, Green) for tops, sides & bottoms.
From 2 each (Purple, Aqua, Pink and Green), cut the following:
    2½" x 2½" squares (20 Purple, Aqua, Pink, Green) for corners.
From 2 each (Purple, Aqua, Pink and Green), cut the following:
    5" x 8" strips (4 Purple, Aqua, Pink , Green)for the sides on the middle.

    Set aside eight 5" x 10" Purple, Aqua, Pink and Green
            pieces for the sides of the head and base.
    Trim the remaining eight 5" x 10" Purple, Aqua, Pink and Green
            pieces to 5" x 9¾" for the top and bottom borders.

Cut the following:
16 Tan 2½" x 5" for arms.
16 Tan 2½" x 2½" for corners.

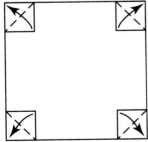

Snowball Block
Sewing the Corners Diagram

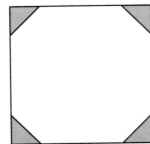

Snowball Block
Completed Corners Diagram

SEW CORNERS OF THE BLOCKS:
Snowman Head and Base 'Snowball Block':
Align a 2½" square of background color with each White corner.
Draw diagonal lines as in the diagram, note the direction of each diagonal.
Sew on the diagonal line. Fold back the corner of the square. Press.
Repeat for all corners.
Trim away excess fabric from underneath.

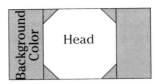

Snowman Head:
Sew a 5" x 10" strip in
the background color to
each side of the head.
Press.

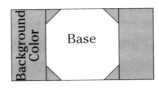

**Snowman Base
of Body:**
Sew a 5" x 10" strip in
the background color
to each side of the
base.
Press.

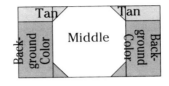

Snowman Middle Body:
Snowman Block:
Make a snowball block
with Tan 2½" squares
on the top corners
and background color
squares on the bottom corners.
Side Strips: Sew a 2½" x 5" Tan strip to a 5" x 8" strip
in the background color. Press.
    Make 2.
Sew a strip to each side of the middle body. Press.

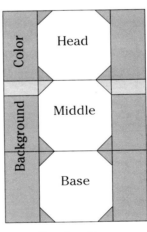

Sew head to
middle body to
base of body.

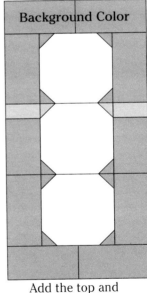

Add the top and
bottom strips.

Snowman Assembly:
Sew the head to the middle body.
Press.
Sew the head/middle to the base.
Press.

Top and Bottom Borders:
Sew two 5" x 9¾" pieces end to end to make a
    strip 5" x 19".
Make 2 for each block.
Sew a strip to the top and bottom of the snowman.
Press.
Each Snowman block will measure 19" x 38".

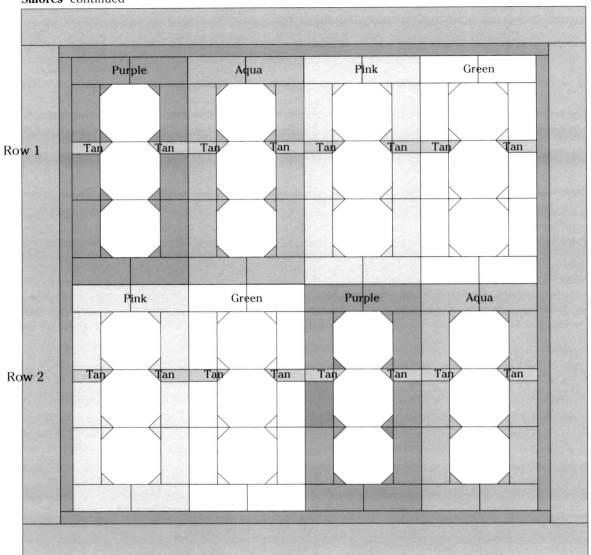

Smores - Quilt Assembly

Buttons & Beads (optional):
After quilting and binding, sew buttons for eyes and shirt, sew beads for the mouth.

NOTE: Do not use buttons on quilts intended for babies and young children. Embroider a center with floss.

ASSEMBLY:
Arrange all Blocks on a work surface or table.
Refer to diagram for block placement and direction.
Sew 4 blocks together for Row 1. Repeat for Row 2.
Press.
Sew rows together. Press.

BORDERS:
Border #1:
Cut 8 strips 2½" x 42" on the crosswise grain.
Sew strips together end to end.
Cut 2 strips 2½" x 75½" for sides.
Cut 2 strips 2½" x 78½" for top and bottom.
Sew side borders to the quilt. Press.
Sew top and bottom borders to the quilt. Press.

Border #2:
Cut the strips parallel to the selvage to eliminate piecing on the long borders.
Cut 2 strips 6½" x 79½" for sides.
Cut 2 strips 6½" x 90½" for top and bottom.
Sew side borders to the quilt. Press.
Sew top and bottom borders to the quilt. Press.

FINISHING:
Quilting:
See Basic Instructions on pages 32 - 33.

Binding:
Cut strips 2½" wide.
Sew together end to end to equal 372".
See Binding Instructions on page 34.

Applique and Buttons (optional):
See page 33 for applique instructions.
Cut out 8 noses from leftover fabric. Applique to the faces in the method of your choice.
Sew buttons and beads for the eyes, mouth and shirt.

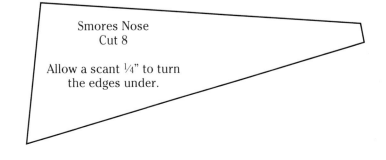

Smores Nose
Cut 8

Allow a scant ¼" to turn the edges under.

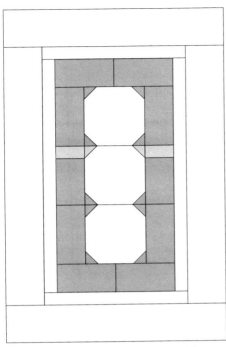

Smores Wall Quilt - Assembly

Smores Wall Quilt
Variation

REFER TO INSTRUCTIONS ON PAGES 29 - 30.

SIZE: 28½" x 47½"

YARDAGE:

Border #1	Purchase ⅙ yd Purple
Border #2 & Binding	Purchase 1⅛ yds Aqua
Backing	Purchase 1⅝ yds
Batting	Purchase 37" x 56"
⅞" Buttons	2 for eyes, 3 for shirt,
Beads	10-6x19mm Black rice beads for mouth

Sewing machine, needle, thread

Border #1:
Cut 2 strips 1½" x 38" for sides.
Cut 2 strips 1½" x 21" for top and bottom.

Border #2:
Cut 2 strips 4½" x 40" for sides.
Cut 2 strips 4½" x 29" for top and bottom.

Sew buttons and beads for the eyes, mouth and shirt.

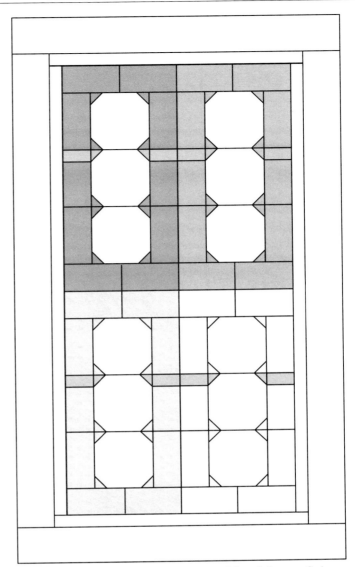

Smores Lap or Baby Quilt Assembly - 1 Layer Cake

Smores Throw Quilt
Variation

REFER TO INSTRUCTIONS ON PAGES 29 - 30.

SIZE: 47" x 85"

YARDAGE:

Border #1	Purchase ⅓ yard Purple
Border #2 & Binding	Purchase 1⅓ yards Aqua
Backing	Purchase 4½ yards
Batting	Purchase 55" x 94"
⅞" Buttons	8 for eyes, 12 for shirt,
Beads	40-6x19mm Black rice beads for mouth

Sewing machine, needle, thread

Baby Quilt:
SIZE: 37" x 74". This quilt is finished. Add the binding.

Lap Quilt - Border #1:
Cut 2 strips 1½" x 75½" for sides.
Cut 2 strips 1½" x 39½" for top and bottom.

Lap Quilt - Border #2:
Cut 2 strips 4½" x 77½" for sides.
Cut 2 strips 4½" x 47½" for top and bottom.

Design Tips with 'Layer Cakes'

I love quilting with 'Layer Cake' collections of pre-cut 10" x 10" fabric pieces. I want to share a few tips for working with 'Layer Cake Squares'. The colors are always beautiful together and create the handmade scrappy look that is so popular today.

My first step in designing is to divide the 10" squares into groups of color... Greens, Purples, Browns, Tans, etc. Next I estimate the number of squares I will need for the center of the quilt.

Sometimes I need an extra square or two of a color, let's say Dark Brown so I look for a Tan print with a lot of Brown and move it to the Dark Brown stack.... and the same with other colors.
Enjoy quilting.

Rotary Cutting Tips

Rotary Cutter: Friend or Foe

A rotary cutter is wonderful and useful. When not used correctly, the sharp blade can be a dangerous tool. Follow these safety tips:
1. Never cut toward you.
2. Use a sharp blade. Pressing harder on a dull blade can cause the blade to jump the ruler and injure your fingers.
3. Always disengage the blade before the cutter leaves your hand, even if you intend to pick it up immediately.

Rotary cutters have been caught when lifting fabric, have fallen onto the floor and have cut fingers.

Basic Sewing Instructions

You now have precisely cut strips that are exactly the correct width. You are well on your way to blocks that fit together perfectly. Accurate sewing is the next important step.

Matching Edges:

1. Carefully line up the edges of your strips. Many times, if the underside is off a little, your seam will be off by ⅛". This does not sound like much until you have 8 seams in a block, each off by ⅛". Now your finished block is a whole inch wrong!
2. Pin the pieces together to prevent them shifting.

Seam Allowance:

I cannot stress enough the importance of accurate ¼" seams. All the quilts in this book are measured for ¼" seams unless otherwise indicated.

Most sewing machine manufacturers offer a Quarter-inch foot. A Quarter-inch foot is the most worthwhile investment you can make in your quilting.

Pressing:

I want to talk about pressing even before we get to sewing because proper pressing can make the difference between a quilt that wins a ribbon at the quilt show and one that does not.

Press, do NOT iron. What does that mean? Many of us want to move the iron back and forth along the seam. This "ironing" stretches the strip out of shape and creates errors that accumulate as the quilt is constructed. Believe it or not, there is a correct way to press your seams, and here it is:

1. Do NOT use steam with your iron. If you need a little water, spritz it on.

2. Place your fabric flat on the ironing board without opening the seam. Set a hot iron on the seam and count to 3. Lift the iron and move to the next position along the seam. Repeat until the entire seam is pressed. This sets and sinks the threads into the fabric.

3. Now, carefully lift the top strip and fold it away from you so the seam is on one side. Usually the seam is pressed toward the darker fabric, but often the direction of the seam is determined by the piecing requirements.

4. Press the seam open with your fingers. Add a little water or spray starch if it wants to close again. Lift the iron and place it on the seam. Count to 3. Lift the iron again and continue until the seam is pressed. Do NOT use the tip of the iron to push the seam open. So many people do this and wonder later why their blocks are not fitting together.

5. Most critical of all: For accuracy every seam must be pressed before the next seam is sewn.

Working with 'Crosswise Grain' strips:

Strips cut on the crosswise grain (from selvage to selvage) have problems similar to bias edges and are prone to stretching. To reduce stretching and make your quilt lay flat for quilting, keep these tips in mind.

1. Take care not to stretch the strips as you sew.

2. Adjust the sewing thread tension and the presser foot pressure if needed.

3. If you detect any puckering as you go, rip out the seam and sew it again. It is much easier to take out a seam now than to do it after the block is sewn.

Sewing Bias Edges:

Bias edges wiggle and stretch out of shape very easily. They are not recommended for beginners, but even a novice can accomplish bias edges if these techniques are employed.

1. Stabilize the bias edge with one of these methods:

   a) Press with spray starch.

   b) Press freezer paper or removable iron-on stabilizer to the back of the fabric.

   c) Sew a double row of stay stitches along the bias edge and ⅛" from the bias edge. This is a favorite technique of garment makers.

2. Pin, pin, pin! I know many of us dislike pinning, but when working with bias edges, pinning makes the difference between intersections that match and those that do not.

Building Better Borders:

Wiggly borders make a quilt very difficult to finish. However, wiggly borders can be avoided with these techniques.

1. Cut the borders on grain. That means cutting your strips parallel to the selvage edge.

2. Accurately cut your borders to the exact measure of the quilt.

3. If your borders are piece stripped from crosswise grain fabrics, press well with spray starch and sew a double row of stay stitches along the outside edge to maintain the original shape and prevent stretching.

4. Pin the border to the quilt, taking care not to stretch the quilt top to make it fit. Pinning reduces slipping and stretching.

Embroidery Use 24" lengths of doubled pearl cotton or 6-ply floss and a #22 or #24 Chenille needle (this needle has a large eye). Outline large elements.

Running Stitch Come up at A. Weave the needle through the fabric, making LONG stitches on the top and SHORT stitches on the bottom. Keep stitches even.

Basic Layering Instructions

Marking Your Quilt:

If you choose to mark your quilt for hand or machine quilting, it is much easier to do so before layering. Press your quilt before you begin. Here are some handy tips regarding marking.

1. A disappearing pen may vanish before you finish.

2. Use a White pencil on dark fabrics.

3. If using a washable Blue pen, remember that pressing may make the pen permanent.

Pieced Backings:

1. Press the backing fabric before measuring.

2. If possible cut backing fabrics on grain, parallel to the selvage edges.

3. Piece 3 parts rather than 2 whenever possible, sewing 2 side borders to the center. This reduces stress on the pieced seam.

4. The backing and batting should extend at least 2" on each side of the quilt.

Creating a Quilt Sandwich:

1. Press the backing and top to remove all wrinkles.

2. Lay the backing wrong side up on the table.

3. Position the batting over the backing and smooth out all wrinkles.

4. Center the quilt top over the batting leaving a 2" border all around.

5. Pin the layers together with 2" safety pins positioned a handwidth apart. A grapefruit spoon makes inserting the pins easier. Leaving the pins open in the container speeds up the basting on the next quilt.

Applique Instructions

Basic Turned Edge:

1. Trace pattern onto template plastic.

2. Cut out the shape leaving a scant ¼" fabric border all around and clip the curves.

3. Place the template plastic on the wrong side of the fabric. Spray edges with starch.

4. Press the ⅛" border over the edge of the template plastic with the tip of a hot iron. Press firmly.

5. Remove the template, maintaining the folded edge on the back of the fabric.

6. Position the shape on the quilt and Blindstitch in place.

Basic Needle Turn:

1. Cut out the shape leaving a ¼" fabric border all around.

2. Baste the shapes to the quilt, keeping the basting stitches away from the edge of the fabric.

3. Begin with all areas that are under other layers and work to the topmost layer.

4. For an area no more than 2" ahead of where you are working, trim to ⅛" and clip the curves.

5. Using the needle, roll the edge under and sew tiny Blindstitches to secure.

Using Fusible Web for Iron-on Applique:

1. Trace the pattern onto *Steam a Seam 2* fusible web.

2. Press the patterns onto the wrong side of the fabric.

3. Cut out patterns exactly on the drawn line.

4. Score the web paper with a pin, then remove the paper.

5. Position the fabric, fusible side down, on the quilt. Press with a hot iron following the fusible web manufacturer's instructions.

6. Stitch around the edge by hand.

Optional: Stabilize the wrong side of the fabric with your favorite stabilizer.

Use a size 80 machine embroidery needle. Fill the bobbin with lightweight basting thread and thread the machine with a machine embroidery thread that complements the color being appliqued.

Set your machine for a Zigzag stitch and adjust the thread tension if needed. Use a scrap to experiment with different stitch widths and lengths until you find the one you like best.

Sew slowly.

Basic Quilting Instructions

Hand Quilting:

Many quilters enjoy the serenity of hand quilting. Because the quilt is handled a great deal, it is important to securely baste the sandwich together. Place the quilt in a hoop and don't forget to hide your knots.

Machine Quilting:

All the quilts in this book were machine quilted. Some were quilted on a large, free-arm quilting machine and others were quilted on a sewing machine. If you have never machine quilted before, practice on some scraps first.

Straight Line Machine Quilting Tips:

1. Pin baste the layers securely.

2. Set up your sewing machine with a size 80 quilting needle and a walking foot.

3. Experimenting with the decorative stitches on your machine adds interest to your quilt. You do not have to quilt the entire piece with the same stitch. Variety is the spice of life, so have fun trying out stitches you have never used before as well as your favorite stand-bys.

Free Motion Machine Quilting Tips:

1. Pin baste the layers securely.

2. Set up your sewing machine with a spring needle, a quilting foot, and lower the feed dogs.

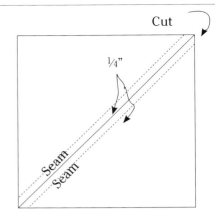

Half-Square Triangle Diagram
1. Place 2 squares right sides together.
2. Draw a diagonal line from corner to corner.
3. Stitch ¼" on each side of the line.
4. Cut squares apart on the diagonal line.
5. Open the 2 new squares with 2 colors.
6. Press. Trim off dog-ears.
7. Center and trim to size.

Basic Mitered Binding Instructions

A Perfect Finish:

The binding endures the most stress on a quilt and is usually the first thing to wear out. For this reason, we recommend using a double fold binding.

1. Trim the backing and batting even with the quilt edge.

2. If possible cut strips on the crosswise grain because a little bias in the binding is a Good thing. This is the only place in the quilt where bias is helpful, for it allows the binding to give as it is turned to the back and sewn in place.

3. Strips are usually cut 2½" wide, but check the instructions for your project before cutting.

4. Sew strips end to end to make a long strip sufficient to go all around the quilt plus 4"- 6".

5. With wrong sides together, fold the strip in half lengthwise. Press.

6. Stretch out your hand and place your little finger at the corner of the quilt top. Place the binding where your thumb touches the edge of the quilt. Aligning the edge of the quilt with the raw edges of the binding, pin the binding in place along the first side.

7. Leaving a 2" tail for later use, begin sewing the binding to the quilt with a ¼" seam.

For Mitered Corners:

1. Stop ¼" from the first corner. Leave the needle in the quilt and turn it 90°. Hit the reverse button on your machine and back off the quilt leaving the threads connected.

2. Fold the binding perpendicular to the side you sewed, making a 45° angle. Carefully maintaining the first fold, bring the binding back along the edge to be sewn.

3. Carefully align the edges of the binding with the quilt edge and sew as you did the first side. Repeat this process until you reach the tail left at the beginning. Fold the tail out of the way and sew until you are ¼" from the beginning stitches.

4. Remove the quilt from the machine. Fold the quilt out of the way and match the binding tails together. Carefully sew the binding tails with a ¼" seam. You can do this by hand if you prefer.

Finishing the Binding:

5. Trim the seam to reduce bulk.

6. Finish stitching the binding to the quilt across the join you just sewed.

7. Turn the binding to the back of the quilt. To reduce bulk at the corners, fold the miter in the opposite direction from which it was folded on the front.

8. Hand-sew a Blind stitch on the back of the quilt to secure the binding in place.

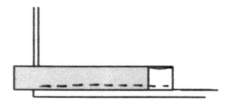

Align the raw edge of the binding with the raw edge of the quilt top. Start about 8" from the corner and go along the first side with a ¼" seam.

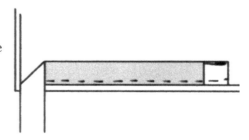

Stop ¼" from the edge. Then stitch a slant to the corner (through both layers of binding)... lift up, then down, as you line up the edge. Fold the binding back.

Align the raw edge again. Continue stitching the next side with a ¼" seam as you sew the binding in place.

Portugal Flowers and Leaves

PHOTO ON PAGES 6 - 7

SIZE: 88" x 88" -

YARDAGE:

We used a *Moda* "Portugal" by April Cornell
- we purchased 2 Layer Cakes
(You'll need a total of 72 squares 10" x 10")

16 Blue	OR	1⅛ yards
18 Golden Yellow	OR	1½ yards
12 Red	OR	⅞ yard
18 Creamy Yellow	OR	1½ yard
8 Green for applique	OR	⅝ yard

Border #1	Purchase ⅝ yard Green
Border #2 & Binding	Purchase 3 yards Yellow print
Backing	Purchase 6⅙ yards
Batting	Purchase 96" x 96"

DMC pearl cotton or 6-ply floss (Yellow, Green)
#22 or #24 chenille needle
Sewing machine, needle, thread

SORTING:

Set aside the following 10" x 10" squares and trim as indicated:
8 Creamy Yellow trimmed to 9½" x 9½" for B.
8 Creamy Yellow cut in half to 5" x 10" and trimmed to 5" x 9½" for Unit #4 and Unit #5.
2 Creamy Yellow cut in half to 5" x 10" for the Cream-Red Unit #3.
2 Golden Yellow cut in half to 5" x 10" for Gold-Red Unit #3.
4 Red - Cut in half to 5" x 10" for Cream-Red and Gold-Red Unit #3.

Set aside the following 10" x 10" squares to make half-square triangles:
8 Red
16 Golden Yellow
16 Blue

HALF-SQUARE TRIANGLES:

TIP: Refer to Half-Square Triangle instructions on page 34.

Pair up the following squares:
4 pairs of Red-Red
16 pairs of Golden Yellow-Blue

Make 40 half-square triangles:
Unit #1:
Make 8 Red/Red
Unit #2:
Make 32 Golden Yellow/Blue

Center and trim each square to 9½" x 9½".

PREPARATION FOR BLOCKS:

Unit #1:
Set aside 8 of Unit #1 Red/Red half-square triangles.

4-Patch for Block A:
NOTE: Refer to the Block A diagram for color placement and direction.
You will need 4 of Unit #2 to make Block A.
Rows 1 & 2: Sew 2 squares of Unit #2 together. Make 16 rows.

Sew 2 rows together to make a 4-Patch for Block A.
Make 8 of Block A.
Press.

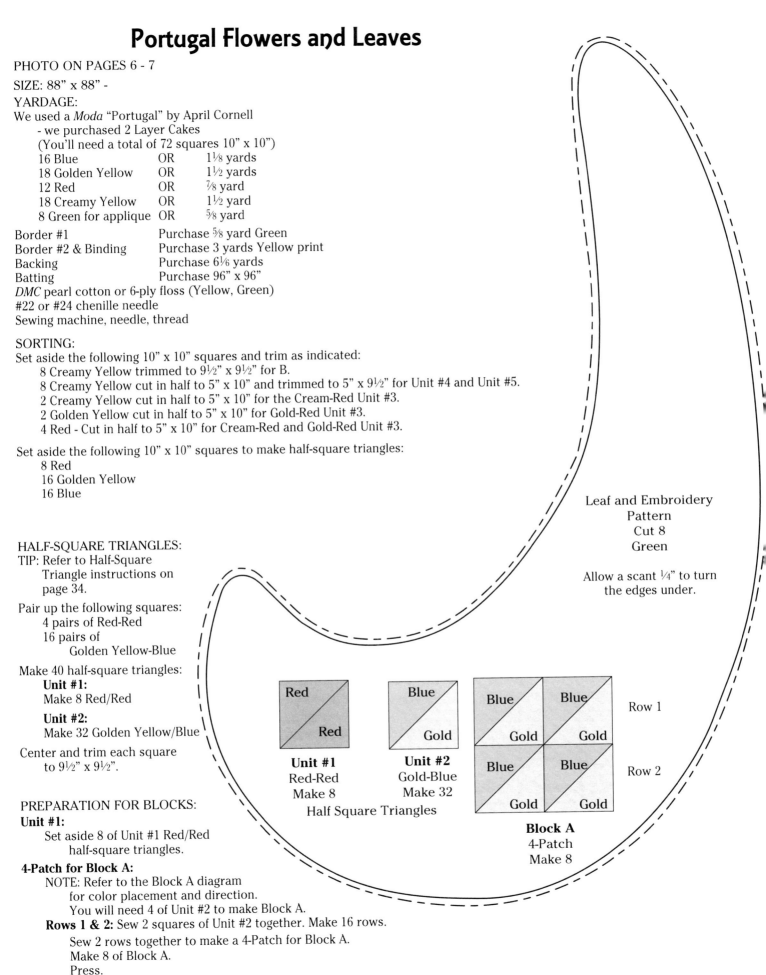

Leaf and Embroidery
Pattern
Cut 8
Green

Allow a scant ¼" to turn
the edges under.

Unit #1
Red-Red
Make 8

Unit #2
Gold-Blue
Make 32

Half Square Triangles

Row 1
Row 2

Block A
4-Patch
Make 8

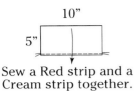

10"

5"

Sew a Red strip and a
Cream strip together.

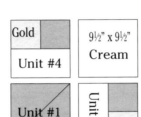

9½"

5"   5"

Unit #3

Unit #3

5" x 9½"

Unit #4
Make 8

Unit #3 - Make 16:
Pair up a 5" x 10" Red with a 5" x 10"
Cream strip.
Sew Red strip to Cream strip to make a
piece 9½" x 10". Make 8. Press.
Repeat for Red and Gold strips. Make 8.
Cut each piece in half to make
16 sections, each 5" x 9½"

Unit #3

5" x 9½"

Unit #5
Make 8

Unit #4 - Make 8:
Note position and color, then sew a Unit #3
to a Cream 5" x 9½" strip. Make 8. Press.

Unit #5 - Make 8:
Note position and color, then sew a Unit #3
to a Cream 5" x 9½" strip. Make 8. Press.

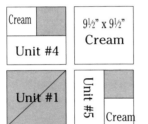

Block B - Make 4

Block C - Make 4

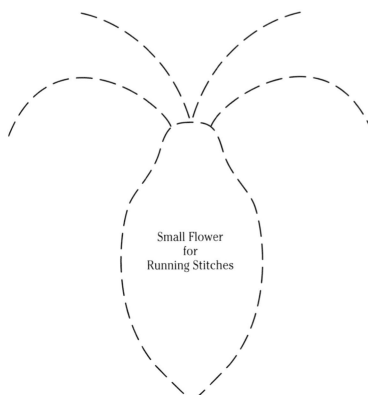

Small Flower
for
Running Stitches

Blocks B and C:
Make 4 of Block B and 4 of Block C.
Block B: You will need 4 of Unit #1, 4 of Unit #4, 4 of Unit #5
and 4 Cream 9½" x 9½" squares to make 4 of Block B.
Block C: You will need 4 of Unit #1, 4 of Unit #4, 4 of Unit #5
and 4 Cream 9½" x 9½" squareS to make 4 of Block C.
Row 1:
Noting colors, sew a Unit #4 to a Cream 9½" square.
Row 2:
Noting colors, sew a Red/Red Unit #1 to a Unit #5.

Sew Row 1 to Row 2. Press.

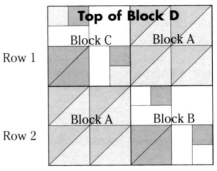

4 Block Set - **Block D** - Make 4

SEW BLOCKS:
4-Block Set for Block D:
Make 4.
Refer to the diagram for placement and direction.
Row 1: Sew a Block C to a Block A. Press.
Row 2: Sew a Block A to a Block B. Press.
Sew the rows together. Press.
Each block will measure 36½" x 36½" at this point.

ASSEMBLY:
Arrange 4 of Block D on
a work surface or
table.
Refer to diagram for
block placement and
direction.
Sew blocks together in
2 rows, 2 blocks per
row. Press.
Sew rows together.
Press.

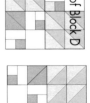

BORDERS:
Border #1:
Cut 8 strips 2½" x 42" on the crosswise grain.
Sew strips together end to end.
Cut 2 strips 2½" x 72½" for sides.
Cut 2 strips 2½" x 76½" for top and bottom.
Sew side borders to the quilt. Press.
Sew top and bottom borders to the quilt. Press.
Border #2:
TIP: Cut the strips parallel to the selvage to eliminate piecing
on the long borders.
Cut 2 strips 6½" x 76½" for sides.
Cut 2 strips 6½" x 88½" for top and bottom.
Sew side borders to the quilt. Press.
Sew top and bottom borders to the quilt. Press.

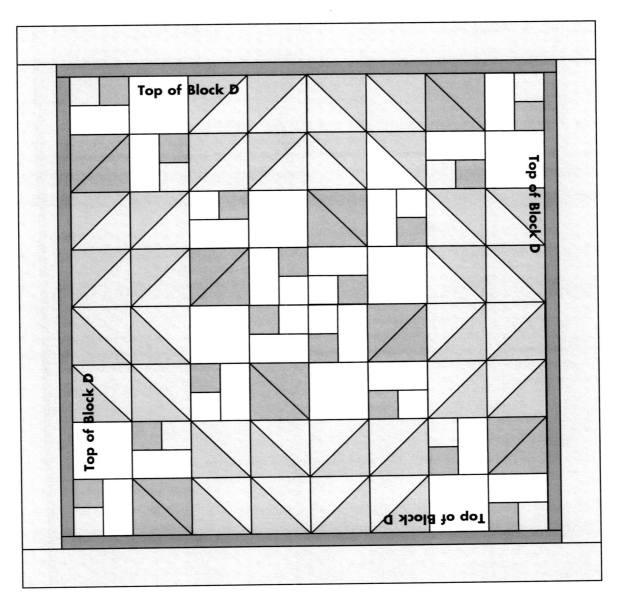

Portugal - Quilt Assembly

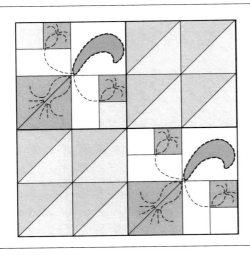

APPLIQUE (optional):
    See Applique and Embroidery instructions on page 33.
    Use the desired method of applique.
    Use the Applique Leaf pattern on page 35.
    Cut 8 leaves, all the same direction.
    Position 2 Leaves on each Block C, applique them in place.

EMBROIDERY (optional):
    See patterns on pages 35, 36 and 38.
    Use a water erasable marking pen or pencil (light lines) to draw
        lines on the red flowers and on the Yellow background.
    Use 2 ply Pearl Cotton or 6-ply embroidery Floss to make
        LONG Running Stitches as accents to the applique.
    See instructions on page 34.

FINISHING:
Optional Applique and Embroidery:
    See instructions above.
Quilting:
    See Basic Instructions on pages 32 - 33.

Binding:
    Cut strips 2½".
    Sew together end to end to equal 362".
    See Binding Instructions on page 34.

Hemming House

PHOTO ON PAGE 43

SIZE: 56" x 68½"

YARDAGE:

We used a *Moda* "Hemming House" by Brannock & Patek Layer Cakes
    collection - we purchased 1 Layer Cake
    (You'll need a total of 40 squares 10" x 10")

11 Ivory	OR	⅞ yard
8 Red	OR	⅝ yard
6 Light Blue	OR	⅝ yard
8 Med Blue	OR	⅝ yard
7 Black	OR	⅝ yard
1 Tan	OR	⅓ yard

Border #2	Purchase ⅓ yard Burgundy
Border #3 & Binding	Purchase 2 yards Ivory print
Backing	Purchase 3¼ yards
Batting	Purchase 64" x 77"

Sewing machine, needle, thread

PREPARATION FOR BLOCKS:

Corner Blocks: Cut 5 Ivory 10" x 10" blocks into 4 squares, 5" x 5" each -
    for a total of 20 squares.

Pieced Border: Cut and set aside 6 Ivory 10" x 10" blocks for
    pieced border #1.

Centers: Cut the following 8½" x 8½" squares for the block centers:
    3 Red, 3 Light Blue, 3 Medium Blue, 3 Black

QUICK PIECING NOTE: You can cut 8 strips 2½" x 5" from a 10" square. I
    use a quick-piecing method that allows me to sew 2½" x 10" strips
    together then cut them into 5"x 10" strip sets.

Strip Sets: Choose 10" x 10" blocks: 5 Red, 3 Lt blue, 3 Black & 5 Med Blue.
    Cut the following 2½" x 10" strips:
    16 Red - 10 Light Blue - 12 Black - 18 Medium Blue

    Cut the following 2½" x 5" strips:
    4 Red - 4 Light Blue - 4 Medium Blue

SEW BLOCKS:

Strip Sets: For each set, you need 2 strips (2½" x 10" of each color).

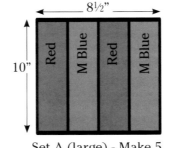

Set A (large) - Make 5

Sew five sets of 2½" x 10" strips
together, alternating the colors,
to make a piece 10" x 8½".

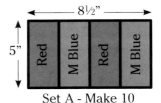

Set A - Make 10

A- Make five 8½" x 10". sets.
Cut in half to make ten 8½" x 5".

A- Red/Med Blue
    Also sew four 2½" x 5"
strips together, alternating the
colors, to make a piece 8½" x 5".

    You now have a total of
eleven of Set A.

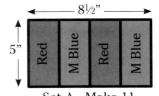

Set A - Make 11

PORTUGAL
Large Flower
for Running
Stitches

FOLD - Center of Flower - Repeat on the other side

Finished Leaf
and
Flower Design

Strip Sets

B- Red/Lt Blue
Make three 8½" x 10" sets.
    Cut in half to make
      six 8½" x 5".
Also sew four 2½" x 5".
    strips together to
    make a piece 8½" x 5".
You now have a total of
    seven of Set B.

Set B - Make 7

C- Black/Lt Blue
    Make two 8½" x 10".
    Cut in half to make
    four 8½" x 5".

Set C - Make 4

D- Black/Med Blue
    Make four 8½" x 10".
    Cut in half to make
    eight 8½" x 5" -

Set D - Make 8

E- Lt Blue/Med Blue
    Make one 8½" x 5".

Set E - Make 1

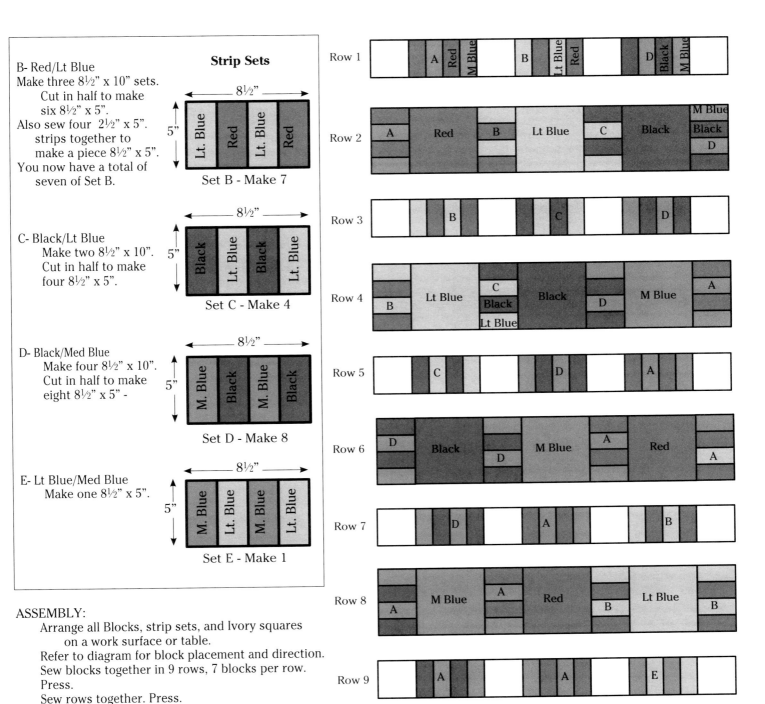

ASSEMBLY:
    Arrange all Blocks, strip sets, and Ivory squares
      on a work surface or table.
    Refer to diagram for block placement and direction.
    Sew blocks together in 9 rows, 7 blocks per row.
    Press.
    Sew rows together. Press.

BORDERS:
Pieced Border #1:
From the 6 Ivory squares set aside previously, cut 24
    Ivory strips 2½" x 10".
Sew strips together end to end.
    Cut 2 strips 2½" x 55" for sides.
    Cut 2 strips 2½" x 46½" for top and bottom.
    Sew side borders to the quilt. Press.
    Sew top and bottom borders to the quilt. Press.

Border #2:
Cut 5 strips 1½" by the width of fabric.
Sew strips together end to end.
    Cut 2 strips 1½" x 59" for sides.
    Cut 2 strips 1½" x 48½" for top and bottom.
    Sew side borders to the quilt. Press.
    Sew top and bottom borders to the quilt. Press.

Border #3:
Cut the strips parallel to the selvage to
    eliminate piecing on the long borders.
    Cut 2 strips 4½" x 61" for sides.
    Cut 2 strips 4½" x 56½" for top and bottom.
    Sew side borders to the quilt. Press.
    Sew top and bottom borders to the quilt. Press.

FINISHING:
Quilting:
    See Basic Instructions on pages 32 - 33.

Binding:
    Cut strips 2½" wide.
    Sew together end to end to equal 259".
    See Binding Instructions on page 34.

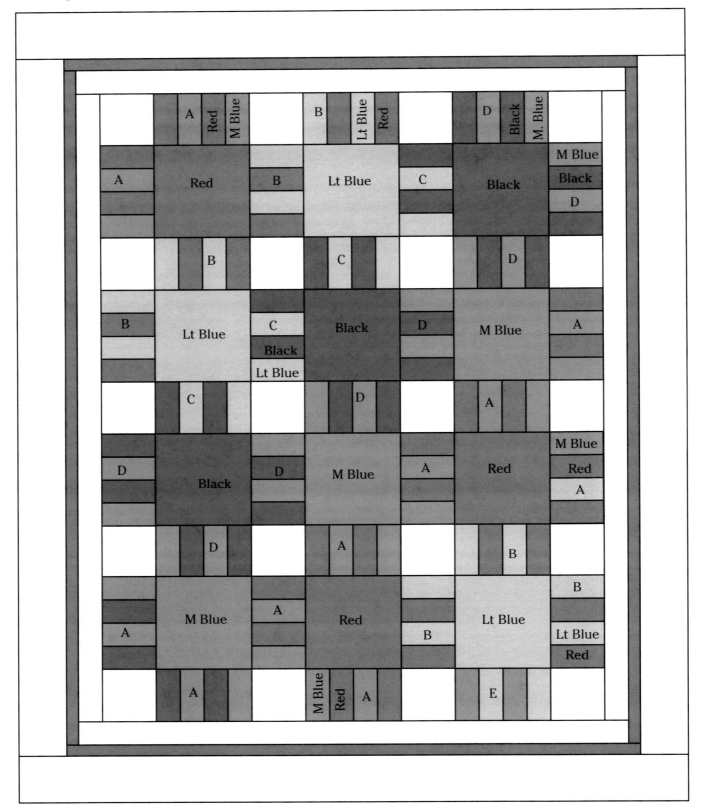

Hemming House
Quilt Assembly

Cranberry Wishes

PHOTO ON PAGE 9
SIZE: 88" x 88"
YARDAGE:
We used a *Moda* "Cranberry Wishes" by Kansas Troubles
    Quilters - we purchased 2 Layer Cake Packs
        (NOTE: in addition, we used the Black border
        fabric to cut 4 Black corner squares.)
    (You'll need a total of 81 squares 10" x 10")

32 Tan	OR	2⅓ yards
8 Brown	OR	⅝ yard
12 Olive	OR	⅞ yard
20 Black	OR	1½ yards
9 Red	OR	⅞ yard

Border #1	Purchase ⅝ yard Medium Brown
Border #2 & Binding	Purchase 3 yards Black
Backing	Purchase 7 yards
Batting	Purchase 96" x 96"
Sewing machine, needle, thread	

CUTTING:

Tan

Quantity	Size	Position
48	4½" x 8½"	16 for Unit A
		16 for Unit B
		16 for Block Center

Brown

16	4½" x 8½"	Unit C

Olive

12	8½" x 8½"	8 for Block corners in Row 3,
		4 for Block corner in Row 1

Black

20	8½" x 8½"	16 for Block Centers,
		4 for Block corner in Row 1

Red

4	4½" x 4½"	Block Centers

Rows 1 and 3 - Make 8

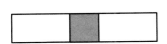

Row 2 - Make 4

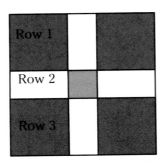

Block Center - Make 4

PREPARATION FOR BLOCKS
Block Center:
    Make 4 Blocks.
    Rows 1 & 3: Make 8.
    Sew a Black 8½" square - a Tan 4½" x 8½" rectangle -
        and a Black 8½" square together. Press.
    Row 2: Make 4.
    Sew a Tan 4½" x 8½" rectangle - a Red 4½" square -
        and a Tan 4½" x 8½" rectangle together. Press.
    Sew the rows together. Press.

Each pair
makes
2 squares.

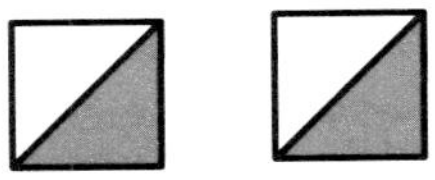

Red-Tan Half-Square Triangles - Make 64

TIP: Follow Half-Square Triangle Diagram on page 34.
HALF-SQUARE TRIANGLES:
    You need 8 Red and 8 Tan 10" x 10" squares.
    Cut all 8 Red and 8 Tan 10" squares into 4 squares 5" x 5"
        for a total of 32 Red and 32 Tan.
    Pair up each 5" Red square with a 5" Tan square,
        with right sides together.
    Draw a line from corner to corner on the diagonal.
    Sew a seam ¼" on each side of the diagonal line.
    Cut apart on the diagonal line to make 2 squares. Press.
    Make 64 half-square triangles.
    Center and trim each half-square triangle to 4½" x 4½".

  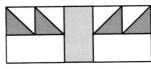

Unit A - Make 16   Unit B - Make 16   Unit C - Make 16

PREPARATION FOR BLOCKS
Unit A: Make 16.
    NOTE: Refer to the Unit A diagram and carefully observe the
        direction of the diagonal and color placement.
    Sew 2 half-square triangles together. Press.
    Sew a Tan 4½" x 8½" rectangle to the bottom of piece. Press.
Unit B: Make 16.
    NOTE: Refer to Unit B. The diagonal is different from Unit A.
    Sew 2 half-square triangles together. Press.
    Sew a Tan 4½" x 8½" rectangle to the bottom of piece. Press.
Unit C: Make 16.
    NOTE: Refer to the diagram for Unit C.
    Sew a Unit A - a Brown 4½" x 8½" rectangle - and a Unit B. Press.

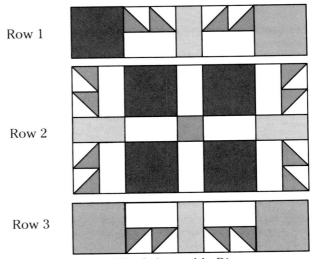

Row 1

Row 2

Row 3

Block Assembly Diagram

BLOCK ASSEMBLY:
    NOTE: Refer to the Block Assembly diagram and note the
        direction of the diagonals and placement of the colors.
    Row 1: Sew a Black 8½" square - Unit C - Olive 8½" square. Press.
    Row 2: Sew a Unit C - Block Center - Unit C. Press.
    Row 3: Sew an Olive 8½" square - Unit C - Olive 8½" square. Press.
        Sew the rows together. Press.
    Each block will measure 36½" x 36½" at this point.

Cranberry Wishes continued

Cranberry Wishes - Quilt Assembly

QUILT ASSEMBLY:
    Arrange all Blocks on a work surface or table.
    Refer to diagram for block placement and direction.
    Sew blocks together in 2 rows, 2 blocks per row.
    Press.
    Sew rows together. Press.

BORDERS:
Border #1:
Cut eight 2½" wide strips on the crosswise grain.
Sew strips together end to end.
    Cut 2 strips 2½" x 72½" for sides.
    Cut 2 strips 2½" x 76½" for top and bottom.
    Sew side borders to the quilt. Press.
    Sew top and bottom borders to the quilt. Press.

Border #2:
Cut the strips parallel to the selvage to eliminate piecing
    on the long borders.
    Cut 2 strips 6½" x 76½" for sides.
    Cut 2 strips 6½" x 88½" for top and bottom.
    Sew side borders to the quilt. Press.
    Sew top and bottom borders to the quilt. Press.

FINISHING:
Quilting:
    See Basic Instructions on pages 32 - 33.
Binding:
    Cut strips 2½" wide.
    Sew together end to end to equal 362".
    See Binding Instructions on page 34.

Hemming House

pieced by Donna Perrotta
quilted by Julie Lawson

Having withstood the test of time, classic design with simple squares and strips are timeless treasures that beautify the decor in any room. Capture the nostalgia of a by-gone age with prints reminiscent of Colonial America in this fabulous quilt.

instructions on pages 38 - 40

Hemming House
'Layer Cake'

Smores Snowmen

pieced by Betty Nowlin
quilted by Julie Lawson

Everyone loves snowmen, especially in places where it does not snow. That's why this quilt comes with an avalanche of alternate choices for colors and sizes.

instructions on pages 29 - 31

Smores
'Layer Cake'

Fresh Squeezed

pieced by Donna Arends Hansen
quilted by Sue Needle

Dripping with zest, you can almost smell the lemons and oranges in this delicious quilt. Certain to be the freshest creation in your sewing room, you will appreciate the ease of assembly this fun quilt has to offer.

instructions on pages 21 - 22

Fresh Squeezed
'Layer Cake'

Natural Garden

pieced by Donna Perrotta
quilted by Julie Lawson

Half-square triangles create pointed petals surrounding each solid block in this naturally serene garden. Adding a border is a great way to dress up an ordinary block, so be sure to remember this technique next time you design your own quilt.

instructions on pages 16 -18

Natural Garden
'Layer Cake'

Birchwood Lane
'Layer Cake'

Birchwood Lane

pieced by Kayleen Allen
quilted by Julie Lawson

Burgundy stars stand out against a birchwood forest bedecked in resplendent autumnal hues. Stroll past gorgeous ferns and earth-tone colors as you assemble the blocks of this magnificent quilt.

instructions on pages 25 - 28